D0933980

**DO NOT REMOVE
CARDS FROM POCKET**

Journey Through History

Prehistory
to Egypt

Translation: Jean Grasso Fitzpatrick

English translation © Copyright 1988 by Barron's Educational Series, Inc.

© Parramón Ediciones, S.A.
First Edition, February 1988
The title of the Spanish edition is *La prehistoria y el antiguo Egipto*

All inquiries should be addressed to:
Barron's Educational Series, Inc.
250 Wireless Boulevard
Hauppauge, New York 11788

Library of Congress Catalog Card No. 88-10380
International Standard Book No. 0-8120-3390-6
Library of Congress Cataloging-in-Publication Data

Vergés, Gloria.
   [Prehistoria y el antiguo Egipto. English]
   Prehistory to Egypt / [illustrated by] María Rius ; [written by]
Gloria & Oriol Vergés ; [translation, Jean Grasso Fitzpatrick].—
1st ed.
     p. cm.—(Journey through history)
   Translation of: Prehistoria y el antiguo Egipto.
   Summary: An illustrated history of ranging from prehistory to the
time of ancient Egypt, with a fictional story involving children to
depict the period.
   ISBN 0-8120-3390-6
   1. Man, Prehistoric—Juvenile literature.   2. Egypt—Civilization—
To 332 B.C.—Juvenile literature.   [1. Man, Prehistoric.
2. Egypt—History—To 332 B.C.]   I. Rius, María, ill.   II. Vergés,
Oriol.   III. Title.   IV. Series: Vergés, Gloria. Viaje a través de
la historia. English.
GN744.V4713 1988
573.3—dc19   88-10380
                                                         CIP
Printed in Spain by Sirven Grafic   AC
Gran Vía, 754 Barcelona
Legal Deposit: B-19.607-88

890   987654321

Journey Through History

Prehistory to Egypt

María Rius
Glòria & Oriol Vergés

CHILDRENS PRESS CHOICE

A Barron's title selected for educational distribution

ISBN 0-516-08475-5

A typical day at the museum...In one of the rooms, a group of people—children and adults—gaze admiringly at the traces of the first people who walked the earth. These men and women were our earliest ancestors. But how did they live? What were their customs? To picture their lives, we have to look at the objects that have been unearthed, and have to observe daily life in primitive settlements that still exist today.

"Why didn't they write about the way they lived?" wonders one boy. "I haven't seen a single book by them."

"Because they hadn't discovered how to communicate in writing," answers his father. "Do you know what we call this long period of time before history began?"

"Prehistoric times, right?" answers the boy. "But look, in those showcases in the back there are some things that seem to be engraved with foreign letters."

"Actually, those are different forms of writing. These things come from Middle Eastern and ancient Egyptian civilizations — the earliest periods of history."

Outside the cave everything was white. It was hard to walk with all the snow, and if people went too far from the cave they might get lost and die in the cold...or be eaten by wild beasts.

Our ancestors, the first men and women who inhabited the earth, took refuge in caves to protect themselves from the cold. In those days the climate was very different from today. Countries and regions where it hardly ever snows today were constantly covered with ice.

"Let's see how lucky we are," said the man. "I've noticed that when I pound these two stones together, sparks fly out that sometimes catch fire on dry grass. If I can make a fire here, we can keep warm and cook some meat."

Making fire required luck and skill. To save the precious glowing coals, prehistoric people used a primitive version of a fireplace, made of flat stones.

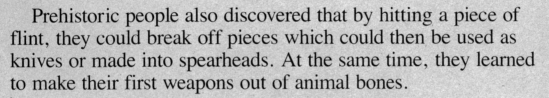

Prehistoric people also discovered that by hitting a piece of flint, they could break off pieces which could then be used as knives or made into spearheads. At the same time, they learned to make their first weapons out of animal bones.

"Ugh! It's hard to get this point onto the stick!" said one man.

"Look how I'm getting one onto this bone! This will be a handy tool for cutting up the meat for the whole tribe!" said his friend.

Since so many stone tools were dug up by *archaeologists*—people who search for and study these ancient remains—this period of prehistory came to be called the Stone Age.

Hunting the animals the tribe needed to eat was a dangerous job. Because they were superstitious, prehistoric people believed that they would be successful in the hunt if they decorated the walls of their caves with paintings of animals. Afterwards, the tribe's witch doctor led a dance in front of the paintings. The people believed that, by doing this dance, the bison and bear would be easier to surprise and kill.

"Look at that bison!" said the witch doctor. "Tomorrow we will get one just as big!"

The witch doctor was worried. In a nearby cave, a group of women and children had died of hunger. Wild game was getting scarce.

Thousands of years have passed since those days, but these fascinating wall paintings are still preserved in caves all over the world.

One of the men of the tribe had died. He was the chief, the bravest of them all. He organized the hunts, always led the group, and knew in which valley the bison could be found.

"I'm going to carry his weapons, so that he'll be able to hunt in the next life," said one boy.

The men who brought home the most food for the tribe were the ones who were most admired. When they died, huge stones were placed over their graves by the strong men of the tribe.

"This way, everyone will know that our chief is buried here," said the witch doctor, raising his hands to the sky. "We will come to visit him sometimes, to offer sacrifices and ask that his bravery pass on to us."

"A baby lamb has been born!" The young boy showed it off happily.

"If the flock keeps growing at this rate," said his father, "we won't lack for meat or milk when winter comes."

"And we'll be able to make cheese, too!" added his mother.

In time, prehistoric people learned to tame animals and to work the land. Thus they stopped being *nomads*—which meant that they no longer had to go from one place to another in search of food. After a while, the first villages were established. Families slept and kept their belongings in huts made of clay, tree trunks, and leaves.

"How different stone and bronze axes are!" said one child.

"My father says he prefers stone weapons," said his friend.

"Mine likes the bronze ones. He says they last longer and don't break, even if you hit them hard. Besides, they're easier to make, and you don't have to polish them like stone axes."

People had just discovered how to melt metals. It didn't take them long to find out that these new materials were very important for them. They make weapons and tools for digging in the earth, cutting wood, cleaning skins....

How did they do it? They would melt copper and tin in very simple ovens. The minerals turned to liquid and mixed together. Then, they poured the mixture into clay molds. When it cooled, the metal took on the desired shape. This period of time is known as the *Bronze Age*.

The left-over grain from the harvest was kept as food for cold spells, bad years, or as a means of trade, called *barter*.

"We'll keep the wheat from the last harvest here," said the mother. "And the milk and water in these other bowls. Where is your father?"

"He's back at the hut. There's still a lot of wool to weave. I prefer wool clothing. The animal skins we've been wearing up to now were so heavy!"

The boy headed toward the river, where some men were hollowing out logs to make boats. He learned that downriver there were other settlements like theirs.

"Perhaps they have boys like me," he thought, "and we could be friends."

"I'm falling, I'm falling! But it's fun to roll on a log." exclaimed the young girl.

"Come on—let's try again!" her sister begged.

The adults in this town did not enjoy themselves nearly as much as their children. They were busy building some cart wheels.

The discovery of the wheel was a major landmark. It enabled people to carry grain, fabrics, vases, and any other objects in carts and wagons, instead of loading them on the backs of animals.

. The products of one settlement could now be carried to far-away places and exchanged for products which the tribe needed. This trade brought men and women of distant areas together.

"Do you know what? I don't like writing very much!" confessed one of the children.

"I'm not having much fun either," answered another. "But if I want to be a *scribe* like my father, I have to learn to write. He is the one who records the merchants' agreements and purchases."

"My uncle, the priest of the temple, also knows how to write. He has to record the stories of kings, battles, and legends."

During that period, few people knew how to read or write. Writing was done with picks, on clay tablets that were then baked in ovens.

The history of Egypt tells us that the rulers, called *pharaohs*, had pyramids built to serve as their tombs. Thousands and thousands of slaves moved and arranged huge blocks of stone that had been transported by boat down the Nile river.

"Poor man! He's exhausted!" exclaimed the boy. "Take this and drink it before the soldiers come!"

The powerful people of the ancient world had slaves at their command who labored in the fields and worked as weavers. Often, sad to say, the slaves were mistreated by their masters, who considered them little more than work machines. The construction of the pyramids, for example, cost a tremendous number of lives.

The Egyptian temples were created to withstand the passage of time. Today, although some of them are no longer standing, their greatness continues to impress us. Inside the temple are the images of gods and the treasure of the priests.

"I'm afraid. What if one of these columns falls?" asked the boy.

"Don't worry. Nothing is going to fall," the boy's sister replied. "Father says that the architects are very clever and that this temple will last ten thousand years. And look at these pictures. The priests call them *hieroglyphics*. They tell the story of the life of the pharaoh."

The Egyptians did not write their hieroglyphics only on the temple columns. They also used *papyrus*, which was nothing more than rushes from the Nile, pressed, dried, and woven together. It was kept rolled up and so was easier to transport.

When a rich Egyptian died, it was the custom to preserve his body so that the remains, called a *mummy*, would look the same in the afterlife as it did on earth.

"The priests have to recite all the prayers written on the wall," the boy said. "That's to be sure the dead man will be happy forever."

"They buried him with his jewels," the girl added. "That way he can enjoy them during his next life. And so that no one would bother him, they will put a big gravestone over the tomb."

Despite all these precautions, archaeologists have only found one tomb intact—that of King of Tutankhamen. The objects found inside it are exhibited in the museum of the city of Cairo, Egypt.

"What wealth!" says one child. "The mask that covered the mummy was made of gold!"

"How beautiful!" says another. "And today we can all enjoy these wonders."

The most important thing we can tell our children about history is that it is about all the challenges human beings have confronted in order to adapt to their environments through time. This daily battle was especially hard during prehistoric times, when men and women had to face a hostile environment.

Fire

Fire was a basic element during the Ice Age. Then the first stone weapons appeared, as well as signs of magic and religion—a response to human defenselessness against nature. These are the phases that we know as late Paleolithic and Neolithic periods.

Stone and Metals

Great discoveries never happen suddenly. On the contrary, people make advances and use them along with old techniques. The use of stone objects coincides with the discovery of early techniques in the melting of metals that were applied later in making weapons and everyday objects.

Agriculture and Livestock

With the discovery of agricultural and livestock-raising techniques, people became settlers. That is to say, they progressed from an economy based on hunting and the gathering of wild fruits and vegetables to an agricultural one where they planted seed, harvested the crops, and saved the seed required for the next crop.

Settlements

Living in a fixed place led to the development of pottery-making and weaving. During this period people used many different natural materials to improve their living conditions. It was the age in which they began to use the wheel and developed some basic navigation techniques.

Early Trade

With agricultural techniques, the first crop surpluses were produced. But a bad harvest or an epidemic could cause a scarcity of basic products. Trade began, based on the barter of surplus merchandise for whatever was needed. Now there were merchants and communication between towns.

The City

The first cities as centralizing nuclei of the economy, politics, and religion rose in the Middle East and in the Egypt of the pharaohs. Great urban formations were created, each with distinct characteristics—some religious, as was the case with Heliopolis, others cultural, such as Alexandria, still others political or administrative like Thebes.

Writing

The introduction of writing permitted the development of commercial life in the towns. The most elaborate ancient writings are the cuneiforms of Sumeria and Mesopotamia and the hieroglyphics of Egypt. The latter were not deciphered until the Rosetta Stone was discovered by the French Egyptologyst, Champollion, in 1822.

Egyptian Civilization

Egyptian culture revolved around the idea of perpetuating life after death. The concept of the afterlife was extremely literal, and corpses were embalmed so that their souls could survive eternally. Huge tombs were constructed and armies of slaves became vital to the ruling bodies of society.